I0151434

Strange Roof

New Women's Voices Series, No. 133

poems by

Catherine Higgins-Moore

Finishing Line Press
Georgetown, Kentucky

Strange Roof

New Women's Voices Series, No. 133

ACKNOWLEDGMENTS

The following poems were printed in the same or similar format in these journals
and anthologies:

Trinity Ball ~ *Heart Shoots*, Indigo Dreams Publishing 2013. ed Ronnie Goodyer
The Escape ~ *Embers of Words: An Anthology of Irish Migrant Writing*, 2012.
Choice Publishing, ed Theo Ejorh,
The empty playground ~ *The Honest Ulsterman*, June 2015 ed Darran Anderson
Delancey Street Daydream ~ *Canterbury Poet of the Year Anthology*, 2016 ed
Abigail Morely, Luigi Marchini, Patricia Debney
First Comes Love ~ *Prole* 2014, Issue 13, ed Brett Evans
On the South Bank ~ *The Stinging Fly*, 2015, Issue 31, ed Declan Meade
Sandymount Strand ~ *Prole* 2014, Issue 13, ed Brett Evans

Publisher: Leah Maines

Editor: Christen Kincaid

Cover Art: John St. John

Author Photo: C. Higgins

Cover Design: Elizabeth Maines McCleavy

Printed in the USA on acid-free paper.
Order online: www.finishinglinepress.com
also available on amazon.com

Author inquiries and mail orders:
Finishing Line Press
P. O. Box 1626
Georgetown, Kentucky 40324
U. S. A.

Contents

"How often have I lain beneath rain on a strange roof thinking of home"

-William Faulkner

Trinity Ball

A bleary eyed young couple
walked
3.5 miles
from Front Arch to Palmerstown Park.
Her
in last night's chiffon frock
protected
from the fresh wind
by an oversized tuxedo jacket,
silver high-heels in hand.
Him
still swigging from a bottle
of Jameson's.
Bow-tie lost
in the rose bush
beside the Graduates Memorial Building?
Love is a piggy-back
over a gravelly footpath,
a home-cooked breakfast,
the whole day spent in bed
with the rose
he picked as fresh
as the moment
he gave it.
Saved
in a makeshift vase
between
Whitman and Joyce.

Balconies

*In memory of Olivia Burke, Lorcan Miller,
Eimear Walsh, Niccolai Schuster, Ashley Donohoe
and Eoghan Culligan.*

Those children of Ireland went to America seeking
the pleasure and promise we are reared expecting—never
from our own strict mothers serving square meals,
dousing suitcases in holy water—but from the East and West
coasts of the land of our dreams. We knew America.
It was as familiar and foreign as a best friend's bedroom.

We never feared it. California was a movie; a Saturday evening
show where the girls were button-nosed blondes called Kelly,
the boys commanded surf boards, drove Porsches, scandalized
fathers. How we wanted to be like them, taking trips to Palm Springs,
limos to Winter Dances and Spring Flings. America meant bigger,
brighter things.

Those six were all of us that ever waved goodbye at Dublin Airport,
fathers lifting suitcases to be weighed. They were all of us who
couldn't keep the shriek from our voices, nor the grins off our faces.
They were all of us, who queued for J1's, planning and plotting
a summer to remember. Their parents ours, holding tight, trying
to keep us forever, hoping and praying they had raised us streetwise

as well as clever. Young. Bright. Happy. Never
suspecting never expecting in such heat
in such mundane pleasure
another balmy Shattuck night would
in a second, steal their light.
Cold comfort to say they went together.

The Park

On Friday evenings a gang would loiter
around the swings, pretending they
were too old for childish things.

They'd slug down cider from fat bottles
passed around like joints. Stumble into
group-watched rummagings

between thorny bushes. Half wanting
to display themselves, half not wanting
to be seen.

On Monday mornings at roll call,
loud whispers of *Slut!* or *Frigid!*
shed chalk marks on the walls. Tears
smudged felt tip on bathroom stalls.

The Escape

A blue uniform in an Orange town.
No safety in numbers, walking home
from school, preparation for later life
in a city where no-one prays.

Colours painted on the crib
remind me I am unwelcome here-
though my father is one of their own
though my home is very near.

Flags and bunting sing of God
and Ulster from terraced houses.
Arches are erected, bonfire wood collected
They start earlier every year.

Grown now and long gone, I give thanks
each Sunday for my new heathen town
where no-one knows, or cares about
the rosary beads my mother packed in my case.

Drumcree

We prayed to Mary
when the Longstone burned,
woke up to cars strewn
across the streets from
the night before like clothes
on a teenage girl's bedroom floor.
Glass glimmering in the July sun,
like pebbles on the shore.

The shops had shorn their fronts,
become beach huts. Wooden boards
where doors and windows used to be.
We watched our classrooms smoke.
Proud pictures turned to cinder ash
under the reporter's foot.

The empty playground

Every November I can't help but think of Mary Lavelle
shivering in her summer uniform, greasy hair hanging
limp not covering those sticky out ears.

Sitting in the playground long after the last bell, after
my mother had taken me to get chips and a new pair
of woolen gloves to match my winter coat

after the teachers had sped back to adult life in their boxy
Ford Fiestas-backseats full of jotters covered in slanted
pencilled essays and miscalculated fractions to be reckoned
with over wine in front of the fire

Mary sat and waited for someone to take her home.
That night she would not tell how the whole class laughed
at lunchtime at her empty slices of hard white bread

as she pulled them from their foil wrapper accompanied
only by a packet of ready salted crisps as a makeshift
filling. How Susan Logan had done high ponytails
for all the other girls *Girls with clean hair Mary!*

They nibbled on Petite Filous from pink plastic lunchboxes
that held Ribena cartons and crustless salmon sandwiches
and cackled when Mary did not come to school the next day.
For her mother's funeral Teacher passed round a card.

Every November I wonder how long Mary sat on those concrete steps,
shivering like a wet leaf, crushing conkers underfoot to kill time.
No-one to button her up. No-one to keep Winter from chilling
her soft, pale skin.

Holloway Road

Holloway Road is where men holler
at women in skirts at 9am. They stand
outside mini-marts smoking in packs
as the women wait for buses, clutching
their handbags, scrolling their phones,
concentrating on ignoring the men
who belch crude laughter, leer
at the Page Three girl, perky
peeking from the newspaper perched
on the bin. The 43 bus lurches forward,
lets the women in. We are grateful
to be smushed against strangers
all the way to London Bridge.

Delancey Street Daydream

On smoggy summer days
half a world away
I wonder if you still play
love songs
and chance your charm
to busk in Central Park.
Last night an ice-cold margarita
burnt my tongue
and though it has been years
since we sat across from each other
in a bar now closed
on the corner of Stanton and Ludlow,
I looked for you.
I thought I'd stop expecting
to see your face
across the table once
the platinum band went on my hand.
Whole years have frittered away
but I cannot throw out the red skirt I wore
to your great pleasure
the night we danced
by the fountain at Lincoln Center.
I can smell the taxi fumes,
the toasted nuts,
the stinking garbage curdling
in black bags outside
the only restaurant
we could afford.
I remember a young couple
sharing a cigarette at 3am,
happy to walk the 42 blocks home,
swanning along Delancey
laughing at the rats.

Unfurling

The bride must unfurl herself like a peony wilting petals.
She must give a petal to her husband, one to her in laws,
two to her parents, saving more for when the hip fractures
and solicitor visits require her counsel, her taxi service,
her homely help.

She will donate countless petals to the children.
They will fall unacknowledged on wet concrete,
lie trampled, like last year's concert posters.
She will slipslide on the confetti of her dreams.

The last of the petals, the ones she never intended to shed,
the ones she thought about pressing, placing in an envelope
as her mother pressed her wedding flowers, gifted them to her
scented with lavender to keep her sweet; those petals will not fall.

They will grow back in to themselves, trying to find the root
of the flower that bore them, trying to turn back time
though they are old now, brittle and brown. Rotten and unloved.
Once their beauty made people reach out with yearning.

It is right the bride changed her name. So different she is
now from the flower girl she once was.

The ward

I
An eight-inch scar runs across
the top of my pubic bone.
The price I paid for a perfect child.
I pray she'll never understand
the sacrifices made in hospital beds-
needles inserted in to me to scratch
the top of her head
to check the dipping heart rate
didn't mean what you fear
from the second
the second line appears.
The long long labour. Two days-
nothing to show for it. The deep stab of
pain. A surly midwife shoving
an IV in to my hand
*The needle has to be this thick in case
you need to go to theatre.*
Did she know even then? Why
did no-one tell us it was all going
so very wrong? Praying hard,
signing my rights away
a teary-eyed surgeon, my age
with a daughter of her own,
agrees to stay.

II
Frantically pushed
into the bowels of the hospital,
'til we reached a sterile room
I hear the clink of tools
being prepared to slice,
move, pull out and push

back together all
that was within me, all
I had worked so hard to protect.

III
No happy revelation after the big push,
not lucid, tired and joyous
staring in to her eyes as my husband
strokes my hair and congratulates me.
Rather, a groggy surfacing
begging for water, finally allowed to suck
on one ball of moistened cotton wool.
The little lamb is placed
next to me. Flat on the bed, I cannot
hold her. My own mother stands by
lest she slide through the guard rail.

IV
Blood pours down my legs, seeps
through plastic sheets as two midwives
lug me up like I am a corpse and they the mobsters
about to throw me over a bridge. They slide
out a catheter I didn't know was there, demand
I piss in a cardboard bucket
so they can measure the urine.
I make it to the bathroom in
centimeters. No-one here respects
doors. They are happy
with the amount of liquid
I have passed. I am allowed
back to bed, not to lie down.
Must stay upright. They'll be back
to check.

I see the scratches on the child's perfect
round head, through the tufts of dark hair
that gave me months of heartburn.
My husband feeds her. They say I might
be able to do it myself
In time.

I am allowed only Paracetamol to soothe
the pain, as though I am in a far-off country
seen on the news, pitied and donated to.
I pray to be put down.
Our beautiful girl cannot make it better.
Too weak to take her, I watch her thrive
in other arms, sometimes have her handed
to me for supervised
but mandatory bonding.

Commuter

Some days, the best you can hope is to travel
five stops not having your body touched. You
can pretend not to hear the lude comments from
the man in the white smock who smacks his lips
as you hurry by, with only your neck on show.

At least you have made it through another full
working-day with only 20% less pay than the man
across the monitor who doesn't have a Masters'
who comes in reeking of Jack Daniels, winking
wrinkling his face like his checked shirt, back-slapping

the boss. The pair of them decided you can take the loss
of a project, only yesterday *definitely yours.*
At least no-one followed you home tonight. Demanded
you get in their car *Slut!* At least you are home now, safe.
You can enjoy a little T.V. before bed.

Gok Wan is on. He's telling you how to accentuate
your waist. Pushing up the breasts of a mother of three,
glaring at her greying bra, clutching her hand as she stands
exposed and tearful in huge hold-in pants,
Gok's stance

—walking naked through a shopping centre will
Change her life! More importantly,
It would make him proud.
The world is full of voices.
Men's so knowing, and so loud.

First Comes Love

At 3am I pace our apartment
praying her colic will abate
so our neighbours don't complain.
I change her full nappy, wipe
creamy spew from her perfect mouth,
but I cannot ease her
red-faced gurning. I hold her up
to our honeymoon photo, a familiar girl
looks back, coquette-ish
over a yellow cocktail.

Our daughter spies me in a frame—
laughing on the lawn outside our old house
in Oxford. Proof. I was there too. I too
took the exams and read the books.
I too wore the cap and gown.
I too had hopes of travel and status.
It was not you alone who planned
for greatness. Don't you remember
how we plotted together?

For this, yes. A blessing no doubt,
but a blessing we planned to share.
Together.
I wonder if the you who got waylaid
before, got lost again
tonight while I am at home, sagging
and oozing, aching from our love's fruition
with only photographs from before
for company.

1994 Peace Talks

They swept glass from their doors, cradled children
through barricades at Holy Cross so their daughters
could learn more than them, while condoms filled
with piss were hurled at their heads.

They bore their children on deserted wards.
Doctors treated the bombed, the maimed
the kneecapped and the kneecapper who
crashed his stolen Sierra and killed a child.

When they bleed out in *an act of God*—they were told
it would have happened regardless of the delay
A student nurse is as good as a doctor.

No Parades Commission, no Victim Support will hear
their evidence. No party will use them as leverage.
No news station will report their loss. They think it never
came to be. She existed only inside…
She.

Their loss will receive no compensation, no
State visit, no commemoration, but all must be
forgiven: The Talks are happening. The world
is impressed by men, sitting around a table.

Registering a birth

The ginger receptionist offers me a seat, smiles
at the little angel, because I am legitimate,
I wear a ring.

He makes the girl in the tracksuit wait,
shuffles paper, checks his phone.
Can't give her a pen. *It's my only one.*

The girl gains a stone of shame on her stomach
where baby weight is etched deeply on us both.
My husband offers his seat.

Shy. She refuses, though I know she must ache
as I do, when she stands. Our children
are no more than a week old.

I coo over her boy. Let her go ahead of me
because the barbarity of labour,
the rawness of my wound, has softened me.

We are comrades struggling to do
all that is expected. Neither knows
what we will be asked next, nor if we will
be able for it.

The Sea Pebble

My sea pebble arrived in savagery. And all in pink.
Some want pink, some blue, others pretend
they want lemon. Blues are too strong, too simple.
I got what I wanted.

When she arrived, she took a lot, then a little more,
then, everything to ensure she was strong, and shiny.
I was powerless. Spurred on to keep my pebble safe
and happy, always happy, no matter the cost.

Not everyone finds a sea pebble. They wander the beach
at home and abroad looking and hoping, pretending not to
search, praying or paying for a pebble to wash up at their feet.

As the people with pebbles go home to frolic under the detritus
of the day, the pebbleless people shimmy, snort, sashay and
sway to some *big in Europe* D.J. The pebbleless people stray
towards the land, rooted in their empty missions, their faddy tasks.

I was once a sea pebble. I was once without a sea pebble.
Now I have a shiny pink sea pebble and it grows.
Though she has the inclinations of a tyrant, I cannot refuse her,
or forget to give thanks the tide was out that day.

On the South Bank

On a crisp winter's day half-a-world away
from the ones I loved, I sat on a bench dedicated
to people who shared this view, once. Who
watched the Thames throwing itself against
the concrete walls, who may too have closed
their eyes, imagined the shouts of children
running through the giant bubble blown
by a man in a t-shirt in December,
were their nephews and nieces.

I thought I saw, amongst the crowds fleeing
the National with scarves and programmes
fluttering, my long-necked mother striding out,
my broad-shouldered father encasing her
in his coat. Fighting the wind which threatened
snow, seeking out a corner snug or bulbous black
cab to spirit them away to a place where the record
player scratched out the Tarantella's rhythm.

What would they make of this place?
The ebb and flow of tourists and commuters-
trainer clad and coffee clutching,
cameras dangling like gothic necklaces?
Hungry for a taste of home, I walked on,
though evening was rushing after me. I
found myself again, on a bench, staring at
the *Portrait of a Young Woman*, more at home
above our kitchen table than in the Tate's
echoing hall.

Missals.

Slid under the pillow to keep me upright
in hospital beds.

Secreted, in the zipped up
lining of handbags.

Nestled between cotton and lace
underwear, there sits Mother Mary.

Pressed in to my palm to watch over me.

I am 3000 miles away from where I first
learned the pride and secrecy of faith.

Mary has travelled with me, in transparent bag,
safe between lavender soap and a diskhaler.

Longstone Lower East.

The Williamsburg Bridge starts, or ends, in the Lower East Side.
It is as if the Longstone broke from a jigsaw puzzle, floated
across the Atlantic, and slid in next to FDR Drive.

Men loiter outside steaming fried chicken shacks. Women with hair
on their chins wheel their wares from huckster stores—selling shampoo,
mops,
chipped mugs. Piss stained pedos wander filthy streets. Shoeless children
hang out of buggies they shouldn't need.

Bowery boasts more bars but the same prompt to women to walk quickly,
protecting their bags, their bodies, watching over their shoulders treading
on tip-toe to muffle their comings and goings, even before dusk.

A sign Drivers! Lock your doors! welcomes Brooklynites to Manhattan
as the RUC warned us on the M1, on the Lower Falls, on the on-slip
to the Westlink. They too reprimanded women for going out at night.
Taxi-men kept rolling, never quite stopping at red lights.

On Clinton Street, there are swimming pools on apartment rooves,
cinemas in basements where realtors host viewings. Silk-effect marketing
booklets boast *Windows! In every room!* Exquisite goldfish bowls
sandwiched

between vegan cafes and cocktail bars rise next to New York's answer
to Divis Flats—shit brown upended matchstick boxes scoring the skyline.
Even we had the decency to tear down flats that stacked people like chickens
in a van on its way to the burn house.

Life as she knew it

She filled her days
with recipes and finding
the right lampshade for the lounge,
a plant pot that toned her kitchen tiles
to the new tablecloth
where the baby porridge
wouldn't stick or ruin the wood.

The house would be finished soon.
She would go back to work,
transition the baby to nursery—
they said it was too early yet
He's only a year old after all.
What was another year? It
goes, and they grow so quickly.

The study was filled with boxes.
It would need repainted in Spring, then
she could hang her prize-winning art
for all to see
she had a talent, once.

.

Numbers

129 wombs collected. 1998 the last time they did it-
if you could believe them. 25 years. A quarter century
and "Doctor" allowed to keep his position, his power
his pension. Off to Spain for some rest and relaxation.
A hard job—wielding a saw on women as they lay,
sometimes tied to a bed, screaming.
Tortured, as they bled and bled,
and bled, not just on the table but still today

from oceans away, from the darkest corners of their rooms
from the dentist chair where the scaler makes a sound that takes
them back, as the roadworks and the digging up the town
takes them back, as the ad on TV for another new horror film
takes them back.

They are back, not in a backroom on their backs
but on the ward for all to watch as they were backed
into a corner. Nurses prepped the tools to the tune of a
tongue lashing from the doctor who told them *move faster.*
His time was precious. His hand were *blessed by the Pope.*

And now not able to open their legs wide enough for
their husbands—a good hot tea will have to do the trick.
Haunted by their symphysiotomies—a Celtic Catholic
cachemar of chaste ideals playing on loop as they drum their laps
nappy-clad under their long skirts, castrated *for their own good*
without consent, or any medical rhyme or reason.

2003. At last. Struck off. But the women in the room?
No. *Only doing their jobs.* Deferred. Prepared, for his hands.
No blood on them. A sordid history. A rotten, filthy, shame.
And now we're known for Savita. And Septic tanks in Tuam.
And the 5000 every year who make for England to do
what Ireland won't. And still, the world will wear green
call us *Colleen* on the 17th, and parade on by.

Damp sets in

Rot and damp deeply burrowed in the old walls
clambered to the surface slowly at first.
It spread like a virus uncontained
sprouting up

in other rooms, patches pressing through
faded floral wallpaper making the house-
a forever home-
unsellable.

Stuck with it, she festered in an attic room pushing
back age and mold with brushes, hanging photo
after photo of children, grandchildren and one
great-grandchild over every green-black bubble.
It would be their job to sort the rubble.

She feared none would come—she bagged her trinkets,
for them. She wrote notes, for them. She kept her gnarled
hands and crackling cough to herself, for them. She left
the address book for priest or neighbor to send word, and
a memento, when the time came.

Homesick

In Berkeley's Bay on a foggy day
I long for the Connemara of 1988,
rolling rain and hills
that slide you down,
putting mud on your skirt
and damp in your lungs.

I miss Dublin town-
the cobbles of Trinity College
paved with Stoker's ideas and Wilde's
whims, smoking gazelles on the Arts ramp
nursing hangovers and new love.

I walk on Telegraph, past the laughing beggar,
remember the boy playing the bugle
in the banana hat on Grafton Street;
the colleen who kept no-one's
circadian rhythm, next to Molly Malone.

Belfast's fickle peace and frenzied boredom-
its marches, road closures and no-go
areas would be a welcome norm
on this too bright Californian day.

I miss Hillsborough, sedate
castled-village of suburbans,
recession proof in Governor's Gate.
Local florists charge per stem.
No chain stores welcome there.

In a Whole Foods south of Market
I roam the aisle of International Food
and cannot find anywhere a Soda farl among the Udon
and Kimchi. I BART back and forth

across the bay spotting foreign objects in
the flotsam and jetsam. A battalion of bottles,
dented cans collect around an uprooted tree.
It reminds of the storm of '91, the fallen oak trunk
we made our famine boat, our QE2, our pirate ship—
all ferrying us to America, the promised land.

View

Green rows of sidelined grass
between the shorn, exposed field.
Clammy day people complained
and sneezed.

Schoolboys climbed the wooden fence
grabbed handfuls of the yield
stuffed it down the back of jumpers,
piled it on each other's hair.

White shirts were scrubbed that night
by mothers alone in kitchens
rummaging under the sink, looking
for a way to remove the stains of the day.

I cannot buy a view like that. A simple view,
a patch of grass, a couple of trees shedding leaves.
I must race like an ant, swipe, and judder, charge
up steps back in to daylight for the chance to sit
in a park between fresh piss, a dog's or a madman's.

Tuam

Septic.
Accepted, suspected
the rotten foundation
of how we treat the women
who bring forth the next generations.

Prison camps really, labouring women labour
in shame, have their babies, taken, renamed.

Decades go by and we try to right the wrong,
mark the territory, lay claim to those innocent
lives lost, as the fifty and sixty-year-old men
and women assert *She did nothing wrong.*
She would have been a fabulous mother.

And you can see in their watery eyes, the scar
of grief—a life lived shuttled away from the one
who grew them.

A dirty secret. Farmed as from a bitch's
litter. Lives can be taken in so many ways.
This happened for years, and decades, and it
happened every, single, day.

Ireland, Church and State, allowed that rotten decay,
those poor dead babies to lay in that ground. A stain
on this nation so profound, we can think of no
word to sum up the horror, except to say Tuam.
Tuam. Tomb.

Tuam.

Sandymount Strand

If there is a place,
        after this,
                I hope it looks like
                        Sandymount Strand.
                  But instead of dogs
          chasing lazy sticks
      and neon joggers
beating the boats,
it will be me
        walking out to you, grinning.
                When the tide is out
                    it will seem as though
                you are caught
          on that stretch of land
      between the bone grey sky
and the foaming water
where only you
      were brave enough to stand
            to let us gather wet sand
                to make the most
solid castle.
          You will be there
      in your Sunday best
    waiting for me,
waving.
    A figure in the distance
        keeping watch
          and waiting.

Catherine Higgins-Moore is a Northern Irish writer based in New York. She writes for The Times Literary Supplement and is founding editor of The Irish Literary Review. Catherine has worked in the newsrooms of BBC Belfast and BBC Oxford. She holds Master's degrees from Trinity College Dublin and the University of Oxford.

In 2016 Catherine was shortlisted for a Pen Parentis Fellowship, the Ted Hughes Elmet Trust Award, and the Canterbury Festival Poet of the Year. In both 2014 and 2015 Catherine was shortlisted for the HG Wells Grand Prize. Also in 2015, she was nominated for Oxford Brookes International Poetry Award. In 2014 she was shortlisted for Cambridge University's Jane Martin Girton College Poetry Prize. Catherine's short fiction has been nominated for the Bath Short Story Prize and The Asham Award.

Her writing has been published in *The Stinging Fly, The Gathering, Embers of Words: An Irish Anthology of Migrant Poetry*, in American journal *Northern Liberties Review*, alongside writers Maya Angelou, Seamus Heaney, John Betjeman and Bob Dylan in *Heart Shoots, The Cherwell, The Honest Ulsterman* and *Prole*.

Catherine's play *Just Two People* was produced at The Oxford Playhouse's Burton Taylor Studio in November 2010. She was offered one of eight places on Columbia University's M.F.A in Playwriting. Columbia's Course Director, Playwright Charles Mee, said of the 2008 intake:

"We admitted a class of unusually bright, talented, interesting, surprising, risk-taking students, and, among them, Catherine is a standout. She is a remarkably smart, gifted, adventurous writer. [Her] work... is outstanding—strikingly original and fresh, beautifully crafted, startlingly accomplished."

Catherine has been awarded bursaries by Kenneth Branagh, and the Mawby Foundation at Kellogg College, Oxford.

www.ingramcontent.com/pod-product-compliance
Lightning Source LLC
LaVergne TN
LVHW091612000420

835510LV00020B/3257